Ghost Forest

MERCER UNIVERSITY PRESS

Endowed by

TOM WATSON BROWN
and
THE WATSON-BROWN FOUNDATION, INC.

GHOST FOREST

Poems

Jack B. Bedell

Mercer University Press
Macon, Georgia

MUP/ P688

© 2024 by Mercer University Press
Published by Mercer University Press
1501 Mercer University Drive
Macon, Georgia 31207
All rights reserved

28 27 26 25 24   5 4 3 2 1

Books published by Mercer University Press are printed on acid-free paper that
meets the requirements of the American National Standard for Information
Sciences—Permanence of Paper for Printed Library Materials.

Printed and bound in the United States.

This book is set in Adobe Garamond.

Cover/jacket design by Burt&Burt.

ISBN   978-0-88146-918-9
Cataloging-in-Publication Data is available from the Library of Congress

*No walls, so the dead
can roam about as they wish.*

—PJ Harvey

CONTENTS

ACKNOWLEDGMENTS

Special thanks to the editors in whose publications these poems first made an appearance:

"Lines for Jean Rhys's Ghost," *Amethyst*; "Ghosts of Birds," *Barren*; "Deus Ex Machina," *Bear Creek Gazette*; "Kate Mulvaney at Marsh's Edge," "Kate Mulvaney Dreams of Breath," and "Kate Mulvaney Sings Along the Bank," *Black Bough Poetry*; "Ghost Fishing," *Book of Matches*; "Storm, Barrier Island," *Bracken*; "The Mysterious Axman's Jazz," *Coffin Bell*; "Ghost Swell, Henderson" and "Lethologica," *Crow & Cross Keys*; "No Stream, Just Leaves," *Cypress*; "Three Knocks," *Deep Wild Journal*; "Cauchemar" and "Kate Mulvaney's Last Breath," *Feed*; "June Bug," *Gone Lawn*; "Gris-Gris," *Gothic Nature*; "Like Lightning from Heaven," *The Haunted Dollhouse*; "Dream: Grabble," *Height Chart*; "Maurepas, Nekyia," *Hominum Journal*; "Dream: Blue Glass," *January Review*; "Tragic Heroes," *Kissing Dynamite*; "Un Baume pour la Journée," *The Lumiere Review*; "Sassaquois, the Old People Know," *Mineral Lit*; "Hungry Dark: A *Twin Peaks* Triptych," *Mookychick*; "Lines for Sonny Liston's Ghost," *Museum of Americana*; "Porch Song" and "My Daughter Already Knows All the Words," *No Contact*; "Kate Mulvaney at Maurepas," *Occulum*; "Kate Mulvaney Calls the Swamp to Hand," *Okay Donkey*; "Dream: Bottle Tree," *Olney Magazine*; "Petrichor," *Parentheses Journal*; "Summer, Orrery," *The Penn Review*; "Lines for Tom Joad's Ghost," *The Phare*; "Kate Mulvaney Remembers Her Father," *The Phoenix Project* (*Second Chance Lit*); "Ghost Forest," *Psaltery & Lyre*; "Demonym," *Random Sample*; "Ghost Heron," *Reckon Review*; "Dream: Minnows," *Rock & Sling*; "Apotropaic" and "Memory: Water-Sick," *San Pedro River Review*; "Acrological," *The Schuylkill Valley Journal*; "Cardinal," *The Shore*; "Kate Mulvaney Births the White Fawn," *The Shoutflower*; "A Kicker's Prayer," *Sport Literate*; "Lines for Dick Murdoch's Ghost," *Stymie*; "Cenote Skull," *Terse*; "Kate Mulvaney Leaves Her Handprint in the Mud" and "Kate

Mulvaney, Shrivening," *The Wellington Street Review*; "Limitrophe, with Cairns," *Whale Road Review*.

"That's Our Waldo" appeared in the Apep Press anthology, *These Poems Are Not What They Seem*. The Kate Mulvaney poems in Section III appeared in a limited-edition chapbook from Belle Point Press, *All the Woods' Wild*.

I. The Gift of Cool Air

Lines for Jean Rhys's Ghost

Well, sometimes it's a fine day, isn't it? Sometimes the sky is blue.
Sometimes the air is light, easy to breathe. And there is always
tomorrow…
       —Jean Rhys, *Good Morning, Midnight*

May every window you pass let in
  a light, Caribbean breeze, and on it
    the voice of God floating

through a sentence you've written.
  May every table you choose
    be the best in the place,

with a fresh highball at your fingertips
  and endless plates of food delivered
    right before you ask for anything.

May you feel free to think of air,
  if air is on your mind, or not think
    at all. Dance and laugh and enjoy

the moon's reflections on the sea,
  tell stories about just that, and know
    whatever hands touch you now

will be as gentle as you wish them to be.

Un Baume pour la Journée

—for Carol Rice

Some days require a remedy—
    the memory of a field so lush
        you could sail across it,

and in the distance, the backs
    of horses, noses dipped
        in bluegrass, steam

rising off their bodies like ghosts
    of family, and always a breeze
        flowing across the porch

so full of Tchaikovsky you could almost
    pour it into a glass. Sip this
        moment. Take a deep breath.

All time is precious. It carries
    hope, even when it must
        drag it uphill, and into

headwind. Accept this salve knowing
    there's nothing out of sort
        that can't be put back in.

Summer, Orrery

On one of the few nights I made it home
    before the street lights came on,

I watched my mother set the table
    for supper through the bay window

on the side of our house. She put out
    plates and glasses for all four of us,

then set out an extra plate and wine glass
    for the empty seat at the end of the table.

She filled the glass up to the brim
    and walked into the kitchen

to put the wine back into the fridge.
    By the time she returned to the table,

the sky had purpled so bad behind me
    I could barely see her outline

through the window screen,
    how she sat down in her normal place,

rested her chin on her balled up fists,
    stared straight at that empty chair

like whatever story it told was new to her,
    and waited for that wine to drink itself.

Gris-Gris

*Yesterday we came into the yard of an old homestead long abandoned,
and we dug up and ate all the daffodil bulbs which were rampantly
growing there. The smell of those people was gone, but something
remained in the air about the ruin of their cabin—something cold and
disheartening.*
—Molly Gloss, *Wild Life*

Even the wildest of beasts
    stay clear of the stench

memories leave in abandoned
    spaces. They might explore

an old farmhouse's cabinets
    for food, or even sleep

in its closets on cold nights,
    but once all nooks are cleaned out

and the yard's dug up
    for whatever it holds,

nature always leaves these ghosts
    to grass and the slow return of trees.

Cardinal

My wife has faith
        red birds are the spirits
                of our kin come back

to visit our days. They fill
        the backyard all summer
                after the grass has been cut,

poke around carefully
        like they're inspecting
                every inch of what we

have left back there.
        She sips her coffee
                and watches them

through the back door glass,
        doing her best to soak in
                all that color.

Once, she called me
        from the parking lot
                at work, crying

through the phone,
        when a red bird landed
                right on her passenger

windowsill. She stopped
        mid-sentence to send me
                a picture of it. By the time

that photo popped up
    on my phone, we'd both
        forgotten why she'd called.

Dream: Grabble

In this dream, my father is wading out
     into the marsh to pick a purple hyacinth flower.

The water's only up to his knees,
     but he's struggling to pull his feet

through the mud. Why he'd want
     that flower makes perfect sense

in this world, so much color under
     gray sky, but I know I'll have to grabble

come morning to understand the music
     these ripples make flowing off his steps.

Petrichor

My mother always opened the window
    after a rainstorm. That breeze

brought all kinds of joy into her kitchen
    and took away the weight of whatever work

she had to get done. She couldn't
    sing a single note, so let her knife

kick up a rhythm chopping onions
    or the hot oil in her skillet hiss out its own tune

while that rain smell just danced around
    the house. Somehow, it was always more

than the gift of cool air on a hard day.
    It was, itself, the whole day.

Now, I can't help but walk the woods
    behind my house after a storm

no matter how many ghosts it raises
    like steam off the hot ground.

Ghost Swell, Henderson

Find beauty, be still.
—W. H. Murray

This swamp never stops breathing.
    Find shade somewhere
        and string up a hammock.

Close your eyes. The bug whine
    dips and swells, water
        laps against the roots

of trees. You'll learn to hear
    distance, the sharp flaps
        of wings. Quiet your mind

and you may even pick out
    claws scratching down cypress bark.
        Keep at this until the sun

drops past the tree line and you'll
    feel the hum of spirits
        gathering on the lake's surface.

Remember, you are always free
    to linger here. Just be still.
        Mind your beating heart.

Three Knocks

It doesn't matter how many times
    I've heard my uncle say
        this sound is just trees

cooling down after a hot day.
    Whenever I set up camp
        at the edge of this swamp

those knocks make my skin
    twitch. I know there's no
        quick way out push-poling

the skiff, and what solid land
    is left would just be a trap.
        Nothing to do but tuck in

like a turtle sunk in mud
    or a catfish under a log.
        Daylight will come,

or it won't, and there's always
stars to count outside the tent.

Lethologica

There's no good

        reason

to swallow

        your words.

Let them float

        past

the tip of your

        tongue.

Say what you need
        to say   now,
because you'll be
        a ghost

        soon

enough.

        Those white shoes

you have on

        look

just like chickens,

        and

there's alligators

        waiting

right down the bank.

II. More Spirit than Thing

Lines for Tom Joad's Ghost

You tell me. How am I supposed
    to show my sons and daughter
        how dangerous it is to stare

into the flames? They look up
    from their Roblox and Minecraft games
        just in time to see a man

stomped out on the TV, a child
    maced by a cop while standing
        on the sidewalk, SUVs

driving into desperate crowds,
    or set on fire in the middle
        of intersections we've crossed

together. The flames dance.
    They spread warmth, embrace
        communities, turn whole

city blocks into campsites.
    So tell me, please. How do I keep my kids
        from reaching out their hands?

Tragic Heroes

—Photographic Print Triptych by Sam Davis, Graphite Gallery,
NOLA 2019

How soon will it be before
    taking our helmets off to admire
            the valley will seem luxurious,

before it's just a matter of minutes
    until we have to breathe
            from our air tanks again,

put our gloves back on before
    the sun and wind peel our skin?
            And when the sand blows

through the valley below us,
    will we remember the sound
            of water?

Maurepas, *Nekyia*

If you've come way out here to see
         what's left of this bald cypress forest,
you've brought plenty of questions
         with you. No doubt, these trees
have plenty answers, but their story
         runs long, and they're in no hurry.
They've been choking on salt water
         since we built levees along the river,
just waiting to show us where our
         logging canals and oil spills are headed.

Stand out here long enough,
         and you'll hear it all—breeze,
bug whine, water lapping in
         and ghost dancing out.
Dry grass shuffles against itself.
         Bare branches point out toward
the horizon. It's all a response.
         Listen. You might even hear
the swamp take its last slow breath
         if you're willing to wait a while.

Sassaquois, the Old People Know

we will never find his bones in the swamp,
    or any part of his hide left under a tree.

He is more spirit than thing, always
    walking in the woods, not

through them, his shoulders
    wider than a buck's rack,

his knock an echo in our bones.
    If he shows himself, it won't be

to help us. He is a warning,
    witness to our wrongs.

He will leave us broken branches
    in the tops of trash oak, warm

nests flattened in the grass.
    He smells the salt on the air,

watches it roll in with the tide,
    feels the tree roots choking,

the saw grass losing hold,
    and wastes no doubt on what we are.

June Bug

The way my uncle told it
    he was a sickly, skinny kid
        before the government men

showed up in their suits
    that summer, carrying
        their big briefcases,

A bright light had screamed
    across the sky and crashed
        into the piney woods over the ridge

that week, and the men
    were stopping at every door
        to find out what people had

or hadn't seen. My uncle
    told them he'd been running around
        out front swinging a stick

when the big light passed
    over, said it wasn't round
        but looked more like an egg

and that it made a flutter sound
    like a big June bug
        before it hit past the tree line.

The men liked that last bit so much
    they wrote it down in their notebooks.
        Before they packed up to go,

one of the men told my uncle
  he could fix the way his ears
    stuck out so bad, though it might

hurt a bit. My uncle had always
  been sorry about the way he looked
    so let the man lay him down

on the living room floor
  to work on him. The man rubbed
    his hands together real fast,

then put them over each side
  of my uncle's head. He said
    the man's palms felt fire hot

when he yanked on his ears
  and popped a crease in them
    to flatten them down. The pain

was gone by the time the men
  stepped off the front porch,
    and my uncle always said

he'd gained a pound a day
  after that and never had a bit
    of trouble getting to sleep.

Demonym

—after *Axe (The Patriarchy)*, a photograph by Susitna Marasul

You've done what you needed
    to do. Now follow the trail

into the woods as soon as the sun
    starts to go down. When the trees

give way to water, there'll be
    no more tracks and you can

take as much time in the shallows
    as you'd like. Throw that axe

as far as you can. The swamp
    loves to keep secrets

and its ghosts are only there
    to dance. They won't care one bit.

Ghosts of Birds

—Antieau Gallery, NOLA

So few bones amongst the stars
                they are like stars themselves
      floating against dark sky,
        their flight peaceful,

                          impossibly
buoyant, featherless.

What could live sparrows do to have us
        honor their dead
                but
lasso our faces with soft rope,
     tilt our gaze toward
        an endless stream of hollow

bones overhead, force us to look away

      from hard earth that blooms
flora
          all the way up to the nape
of our necks?

Dream: Bottle Tree

Last night I sat underneath my grandmother's
　　　mimosa tree, its branches full
　　　　　　of Milk of Magnesia bottles.

Their glass cast a blue dance
　　　along the grass, clinking
　　　　　　in the wind. The old women

tied each bottle there to hold
　　　a wish or a dream or a memory.
　　　　　　Sometimes, they would breathe

a spirit song into the glass
　　　before capping it. Either way,
　　　　　　all the branches swayed

heavy with stories. I didn't have
　　　to turn around to know
　　　　　　the kitchen door behind me

was open to the yard. Inside,
　　　there was plenty flour,
　　　　　　egg wash, busy hands,

chicken parts, and a pressure cooker
　　　heating on the stove. Even
　　　　　　in this dream, laughter glowed.

Cenote Skull

—Chichén Itzá

Before the divers bring the skull
    back to the surface,
they say a quick prayer to Chaac

asking permission to take it.
    With others' bones and jade,
this child had been cast into the hole

to beg rain down from the god's
    hoard of jars. Now, it has
stories to tell of its homeland

and meals. It will be bagged,
    again, and carted to a sterile room.
Clay will wake the ghost of its face

and it will find a place to rest
    its empty gaze.

No Stream, Just Leaves

The days do. They do. They move
    along, come and go. Time is
no river, though. It branches

in every direction, at once.
    I made a poor man's crab boil
last night to bring over

to a friend's house. Its smell
    was so strong my daughter
ran in to ask if I remembered

the time PawPaw chased us all
    out of the house with his boil.
He put so much pepper

in the pot, we had to crawl
    out of the house coughing
like we'd been tear gassed.

He just stood there in the driveway
    smiling loud as could be,
watching us roll around

on the concrete, moaning
    and fussing, begging to catch
our breath enough to move on.

But that day's not upstream.
    I have not passed it by.
I just need to squeeze

a couple of lemon halves
        into my pot, give it a stir,
and stare off at the horizon line

to be right back in it. Or any
        day, even the ones that
brought phone calls so bad

there wasn't nothing to do
        but drop the receiver on the floor
and put hands on knees.

They all jump back on you
        so fast, given half a chance,
it's really no wonder

Lazarus spent most of his time
        staring off into nothing
after he'd gotten his breath back.

III. Enough Blood to Draw Crosses

Kate Mulvaney in Maurepas

The forest is born of water and storm,
    with space to swallow her days.
        She will learn to cure all fevers

with oak moss and pulp from cypress knots.
    Night brings tide moon:
        conjure, locust song.

From the moment she walks the road
    out of town into these shadows,
        she learns to eat only cold things.

People will visit her as long as they feel pain.
    She will coat their shriven brows
        with fish blood, juice of grasshoppers.

When the water off her dock turns brackish, she will
bolt her doors. Her bed is thirst, wet with sweat.

Kate Mulvaney at Marsh's Edge

All swamp fades into marsh eventually.
    Trees turn to ghosts, bushes
        give way to grass and then

open water. The old woman who taught
    Kate to heal showed her how
        to find this edge where

elderberry bushes and wild iris
    grew along the marsh grass.
        She knew the roots of these plants

dug all the way down into the broth
    of life and death sopping
        into everything under her swamp.

These roots, coaxed to surface,
make a bitter tea for the living.

Kate Mulvaney Dreams of Breath

Since the day she stepped off the road into it,
    she has known how the swamp breathes.
        She's felt it expanding and releasing

under her feet, sunk down into it
    in her dreams, taken its water
        into her every hole and crevice.

The swamp's dead swim to her in these dreams,
    deep below its surface. She holds them like
        sunlight, sings away their pain.

For the living, she stews roots and herbs
    pulled from underneath the swamp
        to help them breathe, or stop all breath.

She knows there's no softer thing she can share
with the living, no greater gift from the dead.

Kate Mulvaney Calls the Swamp to Hand

Slow, whole notes draw the swamp's pulse
  right up to her lap. Skinks and grasshoppers
    crawl across the grass, baby squirrels

and rabbits come out from the woods,
  and mosquito hawks float in the air
    around her shoulders. Even eagles

dive out of the sky to be near her song.
  She sings as if her pitch could
    feed the whole swamp, as if

the breadcrumbs she offers could
  heal all need. Her melodies stoke
    the breeze and pull the tides

toward her heart, and all the eyes around
blink in rhythm with her blood.

Kate Mulvaney Births the White Fawn

Under a hanging, orange moon
    she had her back to the grass
        near the tree line

when the white fawn leapt
    out of the earth through the bubble
        of her heart. It burst

into the air as a flash of light,
    stared straight through her,
        and ran into the swamp.

It must have pulled a piece of her
    with it because she could feel
        a tug, always, when it moved,

the only child she claimed as her own,
an echo of her nightly prayers.

Kate Mulvaney Sings along the Bank

At the new moon, she walks the water's edge
      each dawn singing a slow song
            into the crawfish holes sprung up

along the bank. From a boat on water
      you might think her song absent-minded
            and free. When the moon turns full, though,

she'll kneel at each hole mid-song,
          crack in two eggs letting the yolks
            sink down to the swamp's

      gullet. She'll stir mint into each tunnel
          and wait. If her notes hold true,
            the swamp will cough up

catfish after catfish from each hole,
a writhing bounty from its dead.

Kate Mulvaney Leaves Her Handprint in the Mud

Whenever she crosses the swamp,
    she stops every quarter mile
        to press her palm into the mud

at the base of palmettos. She knows
    the swamp's dead will rise up
        toward the warmth she leaves,

the fan of her fingers glowing
    in their dark heaven. Whatever there is
        to learn from these depths

she draws toward the surface,
    prays for it to follow her home
        and spill itself out of the nets

she casts in her dreams, all open-eyed
and mouthing the sharp air.

Kate Mulvaney, Shrivening

Sometimes women from town tie up
      to her dock with a fish still fresh
            from the water. Before they can tell her

what they need, she slices the fish
      from jaw to tail, pulls its organs out
            through the gash, and squeezes

its heart. There's usually enough blood
      to draw crosses on all the women's
            brows, enough twitch left

in the fish to last through her prayers.
      Garfish are best for this, their blood
            old and patient from waiting

in the deepest waters, its stain
thick enough to stay the night.

Kate Mulvaney Remembers Her Father

Something in the steam rising off the berries
        she stews into uncture reminds her
                of her father teaching Greek

to enraptured students. She always loved
        the way his handwriting drifted
                across the chalkboard

in front of his class, the words
        so heavy with mystery, so full
                of portent—σωτηρία

hung up there for all in need,
        scratched onto the board's black slate
                to bring some sign of grace

back into this mist-filled world. By habit,
she raises her hand for permission to read.

Kate Mulvaney's Last Breath

Before the moon can climb above
      the tree line, she makes her way
         to the edge of the clearing,

presses her back against the grass
      one last time, and opens
         her mouth. What she frees

is more air than song, but still
      night birds circle its sound
         and all the woods' wild

draws up to see her spirit
      ride the white stag out
         of her chest, then back

into the swamp, not through the trees
but straight into them, and down.

IV. Nothing but the Shine

Lines for Sonny Liston's Ghost

*Someday they're gonna write a blues for fighters. It'll just be
for slow guitar, soft trumpet and a bell.*
                                    —Sonny Liston

May every sunrise bring you miles
        of downhill road and smooth
                pavement under the balls of your feet,

eggs and plenty steak, hours of
        heavy hands inside the ropes
                and slack jaws to catch them.

May each afternoon stretch
        like the corners of your wife's
                smile toward supper,

and each night be full of aces,
        ice cubes, long rides in the deep
                seats of quiet limos

so far away from cameras and notepads
        you never have to think about
                a bell, or canvas, or the smell

of an empty locker room.
        May there be a slow song
                wherever you've found yourself.

Dream: Minnows

The minnows swim to the end of the cage,
      quick-turn together and swim back.
            Over and again. And I know

this water isn't now, this place isn't
      mine. I can feel my uncle in this dream,
            hear his boat scrape against the dock

behind me somewhere. Breeze, and always
      water so dark the minnows shine
            like sparks below its surface.

Back and forth, back and
      again, so quick I'm frozen
            in my crouch, so close

to the water I know I smell like it,
      know these fish move in swells, blood
            in me, song reflecting off waves,

know in my bones, somehow,
      the broad heads of gar float just
            out of sight—long bodies,

flat scales, more teeth than light
      allows, nosing closer to the cage's
            mouth, my hands.

Apotropaic

—Dunbar Cave, Clarksville, Tennessee

You do not have to go
    far into this cave
        before images begin

to appear along its walls—
    initials, dates, portraits of visitors.
        Then 200 yards in,

near the cave's deepest well,
    two ancient, starburst worlds
        and a warrior floating

face up toward the dark.
    It would be pretty to think
        his weapons' burdens

lifted in this flight,
    if only these signs
        were left for him.

Memory: Water-Sick

1.

I used to dig holes in my backyard when I was nine. I'd start with a garden spade, then switch to hands after four or five inches when the water would fill the space I'd made. I always hoped, like any kid, to find a way to the other side of the world, maybe even meet another boy digging from his own end, just to know there was more world than what I saw.

2.

"This world won't be here when you're my age," my uncle told me at the camp one day after a few Falstaffs. He knew this in his soul, because when he was nine he could close his eyes and see himself in fifty years, steering his own boat in the Gulf, pulling shrimp nets. He knew he'd smell this same air off the salt water, would still be able to tell the sound of heron from egret near shore. There was no reason to fear it would be any different.

3.

"Close your eyes, boy. Take ten breaths and tell me what you think you'll see when you're as old as me. I bet it's nothing, because that's all there'll be." Man, I dug deeper into that dark behind my eyelids with each breath, but there was just no answer there for his "Well?" Nothing but the shine off Uncle's glasses, the sound of wings flapping, and water seeping everywhere around my feet.

Hungry Dark: A *Twin Peaks* Triptych

I.   Nothing Beats the Taste Sensation
          When Maple Syrup Collides with Ham

                    —S1:E4

There's real truth to that, Agent Cooper,
          and to the ice cold of a dead
                    woman's hand. But what fires

could dream-truth light? What pretty
          song would you remember upon waking,
                    and could the steps of that dance

still lead your way? Enjoy your coffee
          while it's hot. Take two sips
                    if you can. And quick bites

of your pie before the testimony rolls in.
          Just keep stacking plates and empty
                    drinks as you go. Your dream soul

will stay on the case. Let him follow
          those tracks left on the road.
                    For sure, you two will meet up soon.

II.   That's Our Waldo

—S1:E7

I wonder what the bird remembers
          when it croaks out "Laura."
                    Does the sound of a flash bulb

pop in its mind as the name begins
          in its throat? Can it feel her cold
                    skin on the bottoms of its feet?

Smell her perfume for just a moment
          before it rolls that *RRR-ahhh*?
                    It has to think about her

eyes. Everyone does. It has to connect
          that name to her laugh. Mynas
                    are smart enough to count.

It knows how many hands
          were in that last room, how many fingers
                    wrapped around her neck,

how many breaths she took
          before the cloth was thrown
                    over its cage, before

everything became stale air,
          hungry dark, and the naked
                    sound of an empty cabin.

III.   This Is the Water, and This Is the Well

—The Return, E8

Spread your smile, girl, and open
        your throat a bit to let the truth
slide all the way in. It will
        fold its wings and swim
tight circles in your belly.

Like the trembling radio told
        each one of us, *Drink full*
and all will end. Swallow hard
        to help. That locust's come
across the desert just for you.

It's waited eleven falls to crack
        its shell and drag itself
through white sand to your
        window, so rest your head.
Let the others bleed.

No need to worry about ghosts.
        The sun will sort them out
in the morning. You've got
        growing to do now with this new
burden, and all it's set to unleash.

Ghost Heron

The old soul wakes in the top of its cypress tree, beak tucked under wing. It readies its bones for flight knowing the sun will stretch fingers over the horizon line soon.

Bare branches let all the cold into its nest this time of year, but the old soul does not mind the way this body creaks. It just pulls itself into the air and climbs high enough to see the sky purple over the lake.

***

Every mile of ground below it reminds the soul of work it's left behind—canals dug, cast nets yanked in full, porches built and weighed down by stories.

Water has seeped into everything, though, and it's difficult for memories to stand up tall enough to be counted.

***

The swamp only flows one way for this old soul. North along the abandoned railway, straight toward a single dock facing east.

The old soul lands softly and steps to the edge of the wood slats to watch the sun rise above the trees again. It spreads its wings wide to catch every bit of warmth the sun has to offer.

***

Behind the old soul, the house begins to wake toward its kitchen. A small boy's voice will beg for cereal, a girl's for biscuits and gravy. A tired mother will pump water for her coffee, put the Dripolator onto the stove, and look out at the sky blooming above her dock.

These eyes on the old soul's back are prickles of ecstasy stirring each feather, but it knows it cannot turn around. Even a stolen glance would turn this body to mist, and the whole cycle would have to be learned again with new bones, earth to sky.

Ghost Fishing

The tired son slogs downstairs for a bowl of cereal in the middle of the night. He just wants to feel the cold milk in the back of his throat and sit in the quiet of an empty kitchen. But right there on the arm of the sofa is the ghost of his dead father waiting for him to clear the bannister.

The old man always loved sitting there so he could look out the front door glass while he told stories. This night he's got a fishing story on loop, and there's no way the tired son can pass up the chance to hear his voice again.

The ghost reminds him of the time they fished for specks off the dock of the family's camp. How they baited the hooks with crawfish and couldn't cast fast enough with all the fish they were pulling out of the pass. Speck after speck piled on the dock until the tired son hooked a fish so small it was almost embarrassing to reel in.

The ghost just shakes his head at the memory of how tiny that speck was and spreads his hands out wide to say it was about that far from the dock when a huge bull red swallowed it whole. And the tired son remembers just how heavy that line got, how the bull red made a hell of a run toward deep water.

The ghost just keeps counting how many hands had to pitch in to drag the whole lot onto the dock. Counts with the same grin on his face the old man had pulling that tiny speck out of that bull red, then yanking that crawfish out of the speck. Just grinning like the whole catch was a big, black top hat with a bottom so deep and full there'd be no end to any of it.

Acrological

My uncle believed you only named a dog so it would come when you said its name. And he never named a dog anything that started with the same letter as any of the other commands he used, because he wanted his dogs to snap to it as soon as they heard that first sound. Never used the command "come" since it wasn't sharp enough to carry, so we always had a line of bird dogs named King or Coop or Crown or Copper. Nothing starting with an S, for sure. God forbid the dog sat down before running in. Nothing with an H, because "high on" actually meant to run off. Couldn't have that either. No Ls. Lying down was not an option until the job was done. Bs were out, too. "Be still" was a big one in the blind. No Ds—"Drop it." No Gs—"Go." It was always good to know, though, that he only expected one thing to happen whenever he said a name.

Limitrophe, with Cairns

On the marsh side of the tree line,
      I walked up on a row of cairns last summer
           stacked tall with rocks from God

knows where, knee-high and perfectly
      aligned with the stand of scrub oak
           guarding the water. The air

on the other side of the trees always
      carried musk, and there was no doubt
           there'd be big tracks scattered

in the dark mud along the bank.
      No way to know it then, but that night
           wind blew water inland from the Gulf.

The flood leveled off right at the height
      of those cairns. And when it backed off,
           it left a smell so hairy you could

almost see its arms full of flat rocks,
      its red eyes fading into the tree trunks
           like warnings you'd have to cross a line to read.

The Mysterious Axman's Jazz

—Joseph John Davilla, NOLA, 1919

When the drummer's stick strikes
        too close to the cymbal bell
in this old tune, ten grocers' ghosts
        hop up out their graves to dance
at the sound of an axe head banging
        on the handle of a screwdriver,

and the ragtime piano drips
        all over the place, its notes
drying in moonlight on Upperline
        and Magnolia. As long as this song
plays, those ghosts will keep stepping,
        their bones shaking in the grave

while the axman passes on by.
        That jazz is the only way
to still his axe, leave it resting
        against a tree in the backyard.
The dogs will howl either way,
        so play on, man, play on.

V. After the Water's Had Its Way

Lines for Dick Murdoch's Ghost

My brother brought me to see you wrestle
        at the Houma Civic Auditorium
                when I was in grade school.

The ring was so small, there wasn't
        nothing you could do but bounce
                off the ropes and meet your opponent

in the middle for an arm bar or a test
        of strength. You couldn't even sell
                punches without falling out of the ring.

I've been to Waxahachie, too, to visit
        my father's people and ask about you.
                Aside from the mill smell, it didn't

look too much like hard living, nothing
        worth hating anybody over. Here's
                hoping you've found some peace

with all that now that you're done.
        Have a cold brew, if there's cold
                where you are, with a Funk or two.

You know, I don't recall how that match
        wound up. Last I remember, you had
                that dude up for a brain buster

with nowhere to put him down.

A Kicker's Prayer

Just let me live in the milliseconds
     before foot hits ball, when all

kicks are good and the wind
     whispers like a ghost

in the stands. I'll tuck into myself
     as Wilkinson did to coil energy,

or I'll follow Carter's sway. The grass,
     my cleats, the tee and ball—

everything aches toward the goalposts,
     and those points just wait to be had.

Storm, Barrier Island

This wind kicks up a mood, song
     and silence, push and lull. And the sky
          settles deep gray over the island,

a heavy blanket for shore birds
     tucking in. There's nothing here
          for shelter, just salt grass

and sand. Nothing to do but lean
     into this storm and wait.
          No way to lock anything

down, no way to block what's coming
     or to hold any of this island in place.
          The only truth here—

water and wind will have their way
     eventually. Pelicans might circle
          the ghost of this place for a while,

but they'll have to make new nests
     somewhere. They know better
          than to lay eggs on hope and habit.

Porch Song

One day I'm gonna die,
and take this whole town with me.
                              —Julia Brown

Wind kicked up as soon as the first
      shovel blade dug into the ground
         the day she died. The way

the old people tell it, oak branches
      started scratching frottoir sounds
         around the bone yard

and you could hear all the hawks
      whistling a tune from the edge
         of the lake. By the time

they got her body into the dirt,
      the storm had already taken
         the lid off the Ruddock store,

blown it right down the street
      with everyone's doors, their shutters,
         and their porch furniture.

It didn't take long for the water
      to swallow everything else.
         And the old folks still swear

you could hear singing in between
      all the gusts, her last breaths
         curling into a hurricane.

Deus Ex Machina

[AM Radio Voice]

I'm fixing to tell you, children.
    That snake you're holding
        doesn't fear the Holy Ghost.

It fears the truth, the flames
    coming off your tongue when you
        speak it, even if the words you use

don't make any sense to its ears.
    You can feel its spine give space
        to your hands. If it could peel out

of its scales to fly away from what's
    inside of you, you can bet it would.
        Right now. Know this, children.

Walk tall in its light. Feel this truth
    glow in you like heat from the sun.
        That snake's told its one lie already.

And it has nothing to offer you now.
    The Great Wind has blown all the fruit
        off its tree, laid it low to rot in the dirt.

Let it writhe in your grasp. Hold it
    close to your face, so it can breathe
        the spirit flowing from your lungs.

[Static]

My Daughter Already Knows All the Words

It's the middle of the afternoon in the middle of the week and the kids have piled into the car to head home from school. Book bags are already open to grab homework and I'm halfway into my son about his World History grade, autospewing stuff my dad used to lay on me about how hanging out with knuckleheads makes you a knucklehead and how life is an EFFORT game and how you are what the numbers say you are and that what you think about yourself won't buy water.

The car is just driving itself west on 190 while I'm spewing, and all my old CDs are throwing old songs around the car that hang in the air like smells you can't even notice anymore when my daughter makes the first sound I've heard all day that wasn't mine.

"Every day I wake up we drink a lot of coffee and watch the CNN/
Every day I wake up to a bowl of clover honey and let the locusts fly in."

It's Clutch, and she's eleven singing along, adding fractions in her math notebook.

"Every time I look out my window same three dogs looking back at me/
Every time I open my windows cranes fly in to terrorize me/
The power of the Holy Ghost/
The power of the Holy Ghost."

Just letting words out like breath.

And I realize there's so many words I WANT to teach her that aren't these. Like how to say "no" so people hear it, how to say "I love you" without it meaning "I owe you." I don't want her picking words out of the air because they're hanging there. I want her to choose carefully, to HEAR and to OWN.

And I want her to be able to say "okay" and mean it. To know the difference between asking and praying.

"Oh this burning beard, I have come undone./
It's just as I feared. I have, I have come undone."

And my son with his knucklehead friends and his grades and the way he just knows he's the smartest thing in the car and my old man telling his old man all this same stuff—she knows this song, too. Heard it every day without having to listen. I just hope it'll come out different when she starts singing it.

Dream: Blue Glass

Last night, I was back on my grandparents' land dragging a pellet gun around like it was summer and I was young enough to have all day doing it. In this dream, there were so many things that needed shooting—copperheads lying on rocks along the creek, blue jays squalling in the scrub oaks, bats diving against open sky—but I wanted blue glass stacked on an old tractor with the sun dying behind it. I carried that want through the whole night, just praying I'd find a bottle to set up on the nose of my grandfather's tractor, catch it just right between its label and cap with my shot, so I could see rainbows spray all over the ground off the shatter.

Cauchemar

Go ahead. Open the front door
    if this dream will let you. There might

be a turtle waiting outside to look
    you in the eyes, or swamp grown

right up to your stoop. No matter
    what's out there, you won't be able

to run, legs way too heavy
    to carry you anywhere

safe. More than a cross to hold
    up, or a clear spirit to save you,

you'll just want a single, deep
    breath, the chance to fill your

chest with some kind of hope.
    If only your ribs would spread.

Like Lightning from Heaven

—Luke 10:17-19

I watch the deacons reach under
    the front pews to pull
snakes from their crates
    and try to see them with
the eyes of a child, always
    certain the next second will
come, without fear of loss
    or knowledge of mis-
deed, fully wide-eyed in awe
    just like these serpents being
held up toward heaven
    and handed to the pastor
for his trial, but I am only
    a child in dreams now,
always dressed in strangers'
    costumes and knocking
on doors for candy or reaching
    into buckets left unattended
on dark front porches,
    stretching my fingers toward
whatever's coiled up at the bottom
    of those spaces, eager
for any sweet, sharp, bright
    gift they might fall upon.

Ghost Forest

—Manchac, after Frank Relle's photograph, *Alhambra*

1.

Backlit by city and refinery's glow
　　these cypress bones shimmer

on the still lake's surface.
　　It's easy to see a storm's

coming with the sky rolling
　　gray overhead and the water

glass-calm. Even easier to know
　　these trees have weathered

some rough winds, their branches
　　here and there, pointing this

a-way and that at what
　　we've done to this place.

Their trunks gather here
　　like hoary, Old Testament prophets

come down from the mountain
　　to rest in this body dump,

gold light hitting the moss
　　all Luminol-shine and whisper.

2.

Water's the only thing
      that gets in here easily, pushed

in by storms or poured
      through spillway gates.

Years of its salt have loosened
      the coast line's faith, turned

forest to roots and sawgrass,
      constant loss. This water

rises, seeps, leaves doubt
      everywhere dirt should be.

It's not worth lying down
      in the hull of your boat

to scrape under the rail trellis
      if you're only coming here

to see what used to be. Do it
      so you can hear the ghost forest

sing about what's coming next
      after the water's had its way.

3.

What is moss if it isn't
        memory? It hangs off these branches,

sways on the breeze like Merton's
        prayers, the closest these trees

will get to needles again. Everything else
        here is dead still, waiting for the storm

to blow in. No frog bellow,
        no heron flap—just moss

waving and the water's slow rise
        to prove this place breathes.

Stillness is faith, locust's whine
        benediction here, and this moss

knows all there is to know
        about holding on, and air,

and how fully empty time is
        with all this water aching

to fill it. Trunks. Branches.
        Sky bruising into storm.

Jack B. Bedell is Professor of English and Coordinator of Creative Writing at Southeastern Louisiana University where he also edits *Louisiana Literature* and directs the Louisiana Literature Press. Jack's work has appeared in *Southern Review, Birmingham Poetry Review, Pidgeonholes, The Shore, Cotton Xenomorph, Okay Donkey, EcoTheo, The Hopper, Terrain, saltfront,* and other journals. His previous collections include *No Brother, This Storm* (Mercer University Press, 2018), *Color All Maps New* (Mercer University Press, 2021), and *Against the Woods' Dark Trunks* (Mercer University Press, 2022). He served as Louisiana Poet Laureate, 2017-2019.